MONSTER MANNERS

In the Classroom

American adaptation copyright © 2026 by North Star Editions, Mendota Heights, MN 55120. All rights reserved. No part of this book may be reproduced or utilized in any form or by any means without written permission from the publisher.

In the Classroom © 2024 BookLife Publishing
This edition is published by arrangement with BookLife Publishing

Library of Congress Control Number:
The Library of Congress Control Number is available on the Library of Congress website.

ISBN
979-8-89359-330-3 (library bound)
979-8-89359-414-0 (paperback)
979-8-89359-385-3 (epub)
979-8-89359-360-0 (hosted ebook)

Printed in the United States of America
Mankato, MN
092025

sales@northstareditions.com
888-417-0195

All facts, statistics, web addresses and URLs in this book were verified as valid and accurate at time of writing. No responsibility for any changes to external websites or references can be accepted by either the author or publisher.

Written by:
Charis Mather

Edited by:
Rebecca Phillips-Bartlett

Designed by:
Amy Li

PHOTO CREDITS
All images are courtesy of Shutterstock.com, unless otherwise specified. With thanks to Getty Images, Thinkstock Photo and iStockphoto.

Cover – mckenna71, Archiwiz, Animado. Recurring – Agafonov Oleg, Omeris. P2–3 – Angelina Bambina. P16–17 – Animado. P19–21 – nik-nadal.

Monsters know many things.

They know how to count and how to measure...

They know how to tell the time and how to read...

But there is one thing that many monsters do not know...

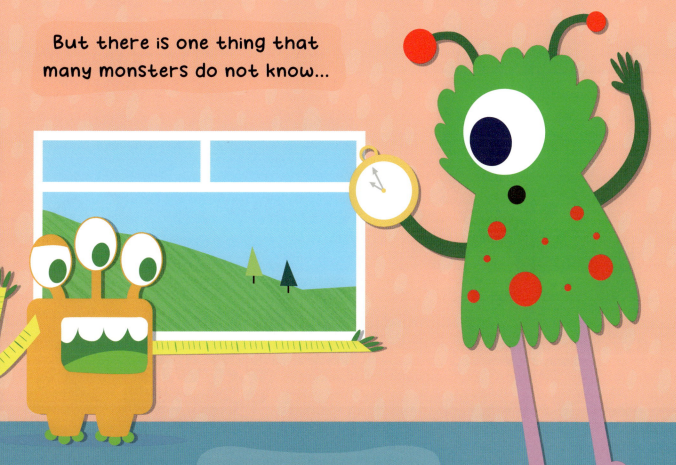

MANNERS!

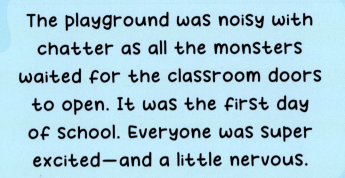

The playground was noisy with chatter as all the monsters waited for the classroom doors to open. It was the first day of school. Everyone was super excited—and a little nervous.

"I heard that Mr. Monclair has lots of rules," one little monster said.

"I heard that too," said another.

Just then, the doors opened. Some monsters whispered excitedly to each other. Others cheered. Mr. Monclair stepped out and clapped his hands to ask for quiet.

"Good morning, students!" he said. "Welcome to my class. You might have heard that I have a lot of classroom rules. Well, the truth is that I only have one big rule: please mind your manners!"

"There are lots of ways to show your manners," Mr. Monclair said. "One of them is to line up before coming into the classroom. Do you think you could do that for me?"

"Yes, Mr. Monclair!" the monsters said. They all lined up by the doors.

"Monsters with good manners show me that they are paying attention when I speak," Mr. Monclair said. "How can you show me that?"

"We can sit still!" one monster said.

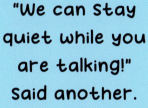

"We can stay quiet while you are talking!" said another.

"We can look at you instead of each other!" said a third.

"Yes, yes, and yes," said Mr. Monclair. "Those are great answers. All of those things show me that you are ready to listen. Sitting still and not shouting out or looking around at your friends can be hard. But doing these things will help you not get distracted while you learn."

Mr. Monclair turned to the class. "Can anyone tell me why monsters with good manners shouldn't shout in class?"

Dot put her hand up high. "If we all shout, no one will be able to hear anyone," she said.

"That's right, Dot," said Mr. Monclair. "We should help each other make the classroom the best place possible for learning." Mr. Monclair began handing out workbooks. "Let's practice being calm and quiet now. When everyone is done with their work, we can have our break time."

As the monsters were tidying up the bits of torn paper, Mr. Monclair suddenly had an itch in his nose.

"Ahhh–"

"Aaahhh–"

"AAAAHH–"

As the sneeze grew, Mr. Monclair threw his elbow in front of his mouth and nose.

"CHOOO!"

Soon, the classroom was clean again. The students went back to their seats. Mr. Monclair looked around. They were all sitting still. He had a big smile on his face.

"Who would have thought that you little monsters could learn so many manners in one morning! You should all be very proud of yourselves."

Stomp put his hand up.

"Yes, Stomp?" said Mr. Monclair.

"Does that mean it is break time now?" he asked.

Mr. Monclair grinned and opened the door to the playground. "Yes, it does!"

The class let out a big cheer.

Not all monsters have good manners, but Mr. Monclair's students do. Do you?

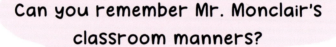

- Line up neatly before going into class.

- Pay attention to the teacher.

- Don't shout out in class.

- Take care of the classroom supplies.

- Catch your coughs and sneezes to keep the classroom clean.